WAITING ON GOD

WAITING ON GOD

LAUREN MILO

Contents

To my parents, for believing in me and in God even when I had lost sight of both.

1

Eight

When I was eight, I asked God for a gift. It wasn't anything special or important but I had learned how to pray in school. I was told I could ask God for anything. So one night I asked God for something specific. I prayed in the way I had been taught and fell asleep trusting that whatever I asked for would be on my doorstep by morning. The next day I had forgotten all about God. Yet, when I went downstairs and opened my door I had the faintest sense of disappointment that something I had wanted had not shown up exactly when I commanded.

2

Twelve

When I was an twelve, I asked God for a gift. This time I prayed ten nights in a row. I had learned that asking for something multiple times meant I could get it. So I asked him ten times and each time I said fervently, "God, please. If you do this for me I promise I'll be good." And on the eleventh day I waited with baited breath. I went to school and couldn't wait to get home to see what I had been given. But what I had asked for had not arrived. I didn't feel disappointed. I felt betrayed.

3

Sixteen

When I was a sixteen, I asked God for a gift. This time I kept the prayer to myself. I didn't whisper it out loud for fear that speaking it into existence would jeopardize its arrival. This time I told no one and I said to myself, "believe in Him enough and it will work out" but secretly I thought, "why am I believing in something I cannot see? I can do this myself." So when my gift didn't arrive, I found a way to do it on my own.

4

Twenty

When I was in twenty, I asked God for a gift. I asked for what I wanted with confidence and brazenness. I demanded it of Him for all the good deeds I had been doing in preparation. I told him I would receive what I wanted and when it didn't arrive, I stopped catering to Him. I had no desire to show my devotion when my God had let me down so often and so much.

# 5

Twenty-Four

When I was a twenty-four, I asked God for a gift. I asked for it half-heartedly as I had gotten used to doing things on my own. I knew I would be let down just as others had let me down before. I made the wish challenging and I made it specific. And when God didn't answer, I felt vindicated. "You see", I thought to myself, "why bother asking when you're not going to get anything anyways?"

6

Twenty-Eight

When I was twenty-eight, I asked God for a gift. I thought, "I will throw a party and make it impossible for my gift not to show up. I will set the stage for God's blessing to be unveiled in front of everyone I know. That - that is what will force God's hand. He wouldn't want to embarrass me in front of everyone I know would he?" And when the gift didn't arrive, the party when on without it. I felt the shame and embarrassment by myself as I alone held the inner knowing that once again I had asked and not received. To everyone else, it was a celebration. To me, it was the final straw.

7

Thirty-Two

When I was thirty-two, I asked God for a gift. I prayed each time things got hard. I screamed at Him when they became unbearable. I cried when I couldn't take anymore. I begged and pleaded with God for the gift I so desperately wanted. Each time I woke in the morning, there was nothing to be found. No great wild change, no earth shattering healing. I woke up bitter and resentful and yet, throughout the day the bitterness would subside. The rage would return to the ocean of anger it had sprung forth from. The hatred and doubt would disappear and I would lay down in bed and once again whisper, "God, help me" because I didn't know who else to ask for when I so desperately needed help.

8

One Day

One day I noticed God had given me a gift. It wasn't what I asked for but it was what I needed. In my life, I had asked God for many things. I asked him for toys and love and friendship. I had asked him for good health and attention and praise. But I had never asked for God Himself; for His power, His love, His guidance to protect me, care for me, guide me. I had always demanded of Him to provide and had never asked to be taken under his wing. I thought that God bowed to my will and I had forgotten that to be under His divine protection was gift enough.

9

Now

Now I don't ask God for gifts. I ask if He will keep me safe from the storms. I ask if He will take care of me in my darkest hours. I ask if He will guide me where I need to go.

Each time I ask Him for something now, He answers.